focus on the family®

THE *Blessings* OF FRIENDSHIPS

Gospel Light

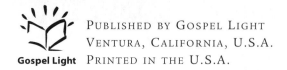

PUBLISHED BY GOSPEL LIGHT
VENTURA, CALIFORNIA, U.S.A.
PRINTED IN THE U.S.A.

Gospel Light is a Christian publisher dedicated to serving the local church. We believe God's vision for Gospel Light is to provide church leaders with biblical, user-friendly materials that will help them evangelize, disciple and minister to children, youth and families.

It is our prayer that this Gospel Light resource will help you discover biblical truth for your own life and help you minister to others. May God richly bless you.

For a free catalog of resources from Gospel Light, please call your Christian supplier or contact us at 1-800-4-GOSPEL *or* www.gospellight.com.

PUBLISHING STAFF
William T. Greig, Publisher · **Dr. Elmer L. Towns,** Senior Consulting Publisher · **Natalie Clark,** Product Line Manager · **Pam Weston,** Managing Editor · **Alex Field,** Associate Editor · **Jessie Minassian,** Editorial Assistant · **Bayard Taylor, M.Div.,** Senior Editor, Biblical and Theological Issues · **Rosanne Moreland,** Cover and Internal Designer · **Jessie Minassian,** Contributing Writer

ISBN 0-8307-3364-7
© 2004 Focus on the Family
All rights reserved.
Printed in the U.S.A.

contents

The Role of Relationships—Back to the Beginning

Women need relationships with each other—that's the way God designed us! Without these relationships we'd be isolated and miserable.

Relationships 101—The Perfect Model

God has provided a model for us to follow so that we don't spread ourselves 500-miles wide and 1-inch deep.

Reaching Out—Encouraging Others

Whether spoken, written or acted out, encouragement is one of the biggest blessings we can offer our friends; and the best part is, it doesn't cost us a thing!

Ready to Reveal—Being Honest and Vulnerable

Scripture admonishes us to bear one another's burdens, to confess our sins to each other and to be honest with others about the state of our heart. How can we overcome the individualistic air that permeates society?

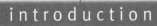

THE BLESSINGS OF FRIENDSHIPS

If a friend calls you with a story of pain or family crisis, will you drop what you're doing to help her through it? Of course—that's what friends do. As you listen to her share her story and weep over the situation, your heart cries as well. But even though our hearts yearn to carry the burdens of others, these burdens aren't ours to bear. Ultimately, only Jesus can bear these burdens. All you can do is cry with her, pray for her, believe in her and rejoice with her when joy comes in the morning (see Psalm 30:5). For that she needs a friend, and friendship is what you can offer.

At a recent gathering of women's ministry leaders, speakers spent a good amount of time discussing the current needs of the Church and brainstorming potential solutions. One of the biggest concerns expressed was the seeming epidemic of shallow relationships among women. In an age when broken families, moral decline and pressures of all kinds are frighteningly high, our God-given support system is extremely tenuous. What happened? Why does it seem like you *know* more people than ever, yet are really *known* by fewer and fewer? What happened to the female support system our mothers and grandmothers enjoyed?

The Blessings of Friendships is a journey back in time, a look back at the days when women honored one another, had time to invest in each other's lives and made a conscious effort to build up one another in righteousness. Perhaps those days aren't so far off after all.

Whether you are doing this study on your own, with a mentor or with a group of women, prepare to find new meaning and fulfillment as you study God's timeless principles about relationships.

FOCUS ON THE FAMILY'S WOMEN'S MINISTRY SERIES

And this is my prayer: that your love may abound more and more in knowledge and depth of insight, so that you may be able to discern what is best and may be pure and blameless until the day of Christ, filled with the fruit of righteousness that comes through Jesus Christ—to the glory and praise of God.

PHILIPPIANS 1:9-11

The goal of this series is to help women identify who they are, based on their unique nature and in the light of God's Word. We hope that each woman who is touched by this series will understand her heavenly Father's unfathomable love for her and that her life has a divine purpose and value. This series also has a secondary goal: That as women pursue their relationship with God, they will also understand the importance of building relationships with other women to enrich their own lives and grow personally, as well as to help others understand their God-given worth and purpose.

Session Overview

The Blessings of Friendships can be used in a variety of situations, including small-group Bible studies, Sunday School classes or mentoring relationships. An individual can also use this book as an at-home study tool.

Each session contains four main components.

Everyday Woman

This section introduces the topic for the session by giving you a personal glimpse into the life of an ordinary woman—someone you can relate to—and it asks probing questions to help you focus on the theme of the session.

Eternal Wisdom

This is the Bible study portion in which you will read Scripture and answer questions to help discover lasting truths from God's Word.

Enduring Hope

This section provides questions and commentary that encourage you to place your hope in God's plan.

Everyday Life

This is a time to reflect on ways that the Lord is calling you to change, suggesting steps you can take to get there. It is also a time for the whole group to pray and encourage one another.

Journaling

We encourage you to keep a journal while you are working through this study. A personal journal chronicles your spiritual journey, recording prayers, thoughts and events along the way. Reviewing past journal entries is a faith-building exercise that allows you to see how God has worked in your life—by resolving a situation, changing an attitude, answering your prayers or helping you grow more like Christ.

Leader's Discussion Guide

A leader's discussion guide is included at the end of this book to help leaders encourage participation, lead discussions and develop relationships.

There are additional helps for leading small groups or mentoring relationships in *The Focus on the Family Women's Ministry Guide*.

THE ROLE OF
Relationships
BACK TO THE BEGINNING

Two are better than one, because they have a good return for their work:
If one falls down, his friend can help him up. But pity the man who falls
and has no one to help him up! Though one may be overpowered, two can
defend themselves. A cord of three strands is not quickly broken.

ECCLESIASTES 4:9-10,12

EVERYDAY WOMAN

Fall leaves crunched under the two women's feet, leaving a trail of yellow, red
and brown confetti on the park trail behind them. Tall aspen trees lined the
path like so many branching crayons, alive with the colors of autumn, while
the last of the warblers and snow geese hurried to catch up with their south-
bound friends. Sonia and Vicky had walked this path once a week for almost
a year now; it was a time they had both grown to cherish. They spent the first
quarter of a mile trying to make rings with their frosty breath; then they gave
up with a burst of laughter.

"So, how's your week been, Vick?" Sonia asked.

"Honestly?" Vicky started.

"Yes, honestly," Sonia replied with an understanding chuckle.

"Well . . . Richard and I haven't held a decent conversation all week, our resident adolescent won't open her door, and I feel like a complete failure as a wife and mother. Other than that, pretty good, I guess." After a pause she added, "I just don't understand how everyone else seems to have it all together. Am I the only one who feels completely isolated? How can Richard come home after a long day at work and only want to watch TV? Doesn't he need to *talk* about things?" Vicky let out a sigh.

Sonia put her arm around her friend's shoulder. "Good thing we still have a few miles to walk, huh, kiddo?"[1]

It's no mistake that our female friends sometimes understand us better than our spouse or even our family members.

1. Describe a time in your life when having a close friend helped you.

2. Why do you suppose relationships have such a great impact on women?

Women need relationships with each other—that's the way God designed us! Without these relationships we'd be isolated and miserable.

ETERNAL WISDOM

To understand why the need for relationships is so intricately woven into our being, let's take a look at when, how and why we were created.

3. Read Genesis 2:18-24. According to verse 18, what was the only thing God mentioned as "not good" in the account of creation?

Even though the primary teaching here is about how God created husbands and wives, what does this Scripture tell you about the need for human relationships?

Matthew Henry wrote "If there were but one man in the world, what a melancholy man must he be! Perfect solitude would turn a paradise into a desert, and a palace into a dungeon."[2] This point comes across in the movie *Cast Away*, which poignantly demonstrates our need for human contact, especially when Chuck Nolan makes a volleyball into a stand-in friend.

Eve was created to be a helper and a companion to Adam, to bring deeper meaning and significance to his life through relationship. Eve balanced the deficiencies in Adam's nature and resolved his solitude. God had given Adam the company of angels and animals, but in Eve God gave Adam someone of his own kind with whom he could truly communicate and share his life—someone tailor-made to complement him.

4. List some differences in the way men and women approach relationships.

5. What strengths does a woman bring to relationships—with men and with other women?

When Adam and Eve sinned (see Genesis 3:1-13), God's perfect design for human relationships was marred. Up to that point, Adam and Eve had enjoyed a perfect relationship with each other and a perfect relationship with God. But as a result of their disobedience to Him, the couple was cursed to spend the rest of their lives struggling within their own relationship and apart from that initial intimate fellowship with God.

6. According to Genesis 3:17-19, what was the curse God gave Adam?

7. Men tend to draw their self-worth primarily from their accomplishments. Knowing this, how do you suppose God's curse affected Adam?

8. According to Genesis 3:16, what curse did God give Eve for her disobedience?

How does that relate to a woman's need for relationships?

Before the curse, Eve drew her sense of worth from who she was in God, her relationship with Him and her relationship with the man she had been created to complement. Adam and Eve even walked and talked with God in paradise before they sinned. Once Adam and Eve sinned, the curse God gave Eve directly affected the core of who she was. Her relationships became troubled. She and Adam hid from God and she began to seek control over her husband (see Genesis 3:8,16). She not only had pain in childbearing, but her relationships with her children also became strained—her firstborn, Cain, murdered his younger brother, Abel, which undoubtedly affected her relationship with Cain.

9. Why do you think God didn't make a world full of men to meet Adam's need for companionship?

Like Eve, women primarily draw their self-worth from their relationships. That explains why the health of our relationships—with the Lord and with others—determines our enjoyment of life. We were designed to engage in meaningful relationships and that is why we feel isolated and lonely without companionship.

ENDURING HOPE

Relationships serve many purposes in our lives.

10. According to Ecclesiastes 4:9-12, how do our relationships strengthen us?

How have you experienced this truth in your own relationships?

11. Briefly describe three of the most meaningful relationships you have been involved in.

12. Choose one relationship from those you listed and give an example of a rough spot you experienced in that relationship.

13. Which of the three relationships you described brought you the most pleasure?

    Which brought the most pain?

    If both answers are the same, why do you think that is?

14. Were these relationships—rough spots and all—worth the effort they took? Why or why not?

15. List some benefits of healthy relationships.

Despite the difficulty we have with relationships—due to the sinful state of the world—they are still a gift from God. We are relational creatures. When we choose to work through the rough spots and commit to loving others the way Jesus taught us to, we will reap the benefits.

EVERYDAY LIFE

Although relationships are a gift from God, we can't go through life basing our worth on them. If we do, we will feel dejected and lonely when they fail—and they *will* fail, in one way or another. The only way to find true and lasting fulfillment is to base our worth on the creator of relationships, God Himself. Elisabeth Elliot put it simply when she wrote, "Where, other than in the will of the Father, shall we expect to find significance, security, and serenity?"[3]

Before responding to the following questions, take a few moments to invite God to open your heart to His leading.

16. Have you ever put a relationship with someone else—male or female—in the rightful place of your relationship with God? Please explain.

    What was the result?

17. In what areas in your relationships with others do you need to grow (e.g., being more understanding, being less critical, being more available)?

18. In what areas in your most important relationship—with your creator—do you need to grow (e.g., spend more time with Him, let Him take control of your life)?

19. Now that you understand the role that relationships play in your life as a woman created by God, what steps will you take this week to strengthen the core relationships you have?

Dear Father, thank You for creating me to be the perfect complement to man's masculinity and for giving me the ability to encourage other women. As I continue to learn Your design for right relationships, teach me to find my true fulfillment in You alone. May my relationship with You far surpass anything I could ever imagine. Amen.

Notes

1. This story is a fictional account. Any resemblance to actual events or people, living or dead, is purely coincidental.
2. Matthew Henry, *Commentary on the Whole Bible* (Grand Rapids, MI: Zondervan Publishing House, 1986), n.p.
3. Elisabeth Elliot, *Keep a Quiet Heart* (New York: Walker and Company, 1999), n.p.

RELATIONSHIPS *101*

THE PERFECT MODEL

*A man of many companions may come to ruin, but there is a
friend who sticks closer than a brother.*

PROVERBS 18:24

E V E R Y D A Y   W O M A N

The feathery softness of the down comforter caused Marissa's tired body to
relax ever so slightly. After an extremely long day, the bed was a welcome lux-
ury. As Marissa looked over at the leather-covered Bible on her nightstand,
the green neon 10:45 showing on the clock sitting next to the Bible con-
firmed what her tired body already knew: It was late. *Lord, You understand,
right? I'm so exhausted!*

Marissa reached over the Bible and switched off the lamp, and the room
filled with silent, still darkness. As she lay there, Marissa's mind raced with
thoughts. One by one, the seemingly hundreds of people with whom she had
conversed during the day came back to tell their stories again, like a late-
night talk show, in which Marissa played host, counselor and chaplain. That
morning, she had befriended the new woman at the single's class at church;
then she had lunch with some friends from the class. The afternoon had
been spent with a high school girl whom Marissa had been mentoring, who

needed a lot of direction. Next had been an early dinner with an old friend from high school, and then back to church for the evening service. After teaching a class at that service, she had coffee with several of her students at the local coffee shop. Two hours and a mocha cappuccino later, Marissa drove home, emotionally and physically drained. She couldn't wait to crawl into bed.

As she pulled the comforter up around her, she realized how overwhelmed she felt. *Lord,* she began to pray silently, *You were proud of me today, right? I'm a good friend; I really care about people and I do my best to show it.*

As she continued to think about her day and the people with whom she had spent time, she still had the nagging feeling that something wasn't right. Then it occurred to her: How could she spend her whole day investing in friendships yet neglect her most important one? Reluctantly, she turned the light back on. Through squinting, tired eyes, she pulled the leather Bible from the nightstand and opened it.[1]

E-mail, free weekend minutes, frequent-flyer miles, dial-10-10, ad nauseam—it's no wonder we feel more pressure to maintain more relationships than ever before. We are involved in more activities that take us farther from home than generations past; we are encouraged by our churches to stay involved in relational ministries; and those of us who have children find yet another avenue for relationships through sports and school activities in which our kids are involved! All these opportunities for relationships, yet we still have the same 24 hours in each day, along with the same finite energy resources. Sounds like a recipe for serious burnout, doesn't it?

Without some guidelines, we will spread ourselves 500-miles wide and 1-inch deep. But God has called us to nurture one another, and as we've already seen, women are wired to need relationships—so what can we do?

1. At the end of the day have you ever felt the same way Marissa felt? Please explain.

2. Use the following scale to show how often you feel overwhelmed by the volume of relationships in which you are involved:

1	2	3	4	5	6	7	8	9	10

Never   Sometimes   Always

Believe it or not, God doesn't want us to feel like we're drowning in a relational whirlpool. So, He has provided a relationship model for us to follow.

ETERNAL WISDOM

Ironically, the biggest hindrance to meaningful relationships is an overabundance of them! When we spread ourselves too thin relationally, we won't be able to go as deep as we need to go—to the depth where we are vulnerable and receive the accountability and support we need. So what is the answer? Are we to dump half our friends (since we can't dump our family members!)? No! What we can do is learn to balance meaningful relationships with the other tasks God has called us to complete.

Let's take a look at how Jesus chose to invest in the lives of those with whom He came into contact.

The Crowds

Of Jesus' 33 years on Earth, only 3 were spent in public ministry. During those 3 years, news of His miracles and teaching spread, and crowds formed wherever He went. Though Jesus invested time and energy in the people who gathered, they did not receive the bulk of His time or energy.

3. Read the following passages. What does each tell us about Jesus' ministry to the crowds?

Matthew 7:28-29

Matthew 9:35-36

Matthew 13:34

4. According to Matthew 13:34-43, how did Jesus treat the crowds differently from the way He treated His disciples?

Though Jesus loved the multitudes that flocked to see Him, He reserved the best part of Himself for those He was training for ministry.

The Seventy-Two

Of the thousands of people who gathered around Him, Jesus chose only 72 (some manuscripts say 70) to send ahead of Him during His final journey to Jerusalem (see Luke 10:1). These followers had likely heard Jesus speak the same parables many times and believed that Jesus was who He said He was. Although these followers were given the power to cast out demons in Jesus' name (see Luke 10:17), they were not in Jesus' inner circle of disciples.

5. Why do you think Jesus didn't spend as much time with these believers—even though they may have been as committed to Him—as He did with His 12 disciples?

The Twelve

"The Twelve"—that phrase probably brings to mind the many stories of Jesus and His closest friends, the 12 disciples. Sometimes they fouled things up; sometimes they amused Jesus with their childish antics; sometimes they bickered and argued with one another—but they were always with Him.

And though they didn't fully comprehend what Jesus had come to do, they boldly professed that they would die for Him if necessary. Jesus knew them intimately—He knew their quirks, their strengths and their weaknesses—and they in turn saw a side of Jesus no others saw.

6. What did Jesus tell His disciples privately in Luke 10:23-24?

    Why do you think Jesus said this only to the Twelve after having addressed the 72 in Luke 10:1-22?

7. According to Luke 9:1-6, how did the disciples know what to preach in the towns they entered?

The primary thrust of Jesus' ministry was toward these dozen men. He had been training the Twelve all along to advance the kingdom of God when He returned to heaven. Practically speaking, it was a perfect strategy. The number of people Jesus was able to reach—while on Earth and after—was increased a hundredfold by choosing to mentor only a few. He taught the disciples how to imitate Him so that each of them would be able to go out and reach hundreds. But Jesus didn't teach the Twelve just to increase the numbers—even though He was fully God, He was also fully human; and as such, He was limited by time and energy constraints just like you and me.

8. What would have happened if Jesus tried to spend equal amounts of time with every person with whom He came into contact?

9. What benefits did Jesus receive from investing the majority of His time and energy in a handful of followers?

The Three

Though Jesus loved each one of His 12 disciples dearly, even He had His favorites—those to whom He felt closest.

10. In Luke 9:28-36, which three disciples were allowed to catch a glimpse of Jesus' glory?

    Why do you suppose Jesus chose these three disciples for this honor?

    Why do you suppose they didn't tell anyone else about the experience?

11. According to Mark 14:32-34, at what other event were these same three disciples singled out by Jesus? Why do you suppose He took them and not the others?

Jesus Christ loved all of His disciples, but Peter, James and John seemed to be especially dear to Him. In human relationships, it is only natural to feel more affection for some people than for others. Many different factors contribute to this feeling, including personality, commonalities and shared experiences.

12. Name someone in your life who's been an especially dear friend to you.

What drew you to that person?

13. What are some of the benefits of having a core group of three or four close friends?

ENDURING HOPE

No matter the number of relationships you may be juggling, the way Christ handled His relationships serves as an excellent example of how to prioritize yours. Like the crowds who surrounded Jesus, you probably have many acquaintances—people who you know by name but with whom you don't invest the time or energy to develop relationships. Although you are not close to these people, you can still be an encouragement and an example to them by the way you live your life.

Like Jesus' 72, there are probably others in your life with whom you formally relate (such as in a Sunday School class or work setting) or with whom you occasionally spend time. These people are more than acquaintances, but you do not consider them close friends.

Your inner circle—your 12—are those friends with whom you "do life." You have made a choice to invest your time and energy into these relationships. Phone calls and visits occur with regularity, and you make it a point to be there to support each other during rough times. These friends know they can count on you when the going gets tough.

14. Which women in your life now would fall under this category of the 12?

Your core group of friends comprises those especially dear friends—those for whom you have a special affinity. You can bare your soul to these friends. They will hold you accountable, they will teach and encourage you, and they will fill your need for deeper relationships. These friends laugh with you, cry with you, argue with you and challenge you—they love you in spite of your faults.

15. Who would you consider to be your core group of friends?

What would happen if you tried to include everyone you know in this inner circle?

Each relationship God brings to your life has its place. Jesus demonstrated this, and He showed us that not all relationships in our lives are going to go beyond the level of a casual acquaintance; fewer still will become casual friendships and only a select few will comprise our inner circle. This is our built-in mechanism for managing our finite time and energy.

16. What purposes for woman-to-woman friendships are given in Titus 2:4-5?

What additional reason for relationships is given in Hebrews 10:24-25?

EVERYDAY LIFE

Your circle of friends is fluid, not static—in other words, it *will* change! As mentioned earlier, Jesus invested in the crowds, the 72, the disciples and His inner core of followers only during His three years of visible ministry. Before that, He likely had a much smaller circle of friends from His hometown, from His work as a craftsman, etc.

17. What circumstances could cause the group of friends you have now to change?

We can't predict what the future holds, but it's important to commit to our friends for whatever time period God grants our friendships. Those really deep relationships that fulfill, encourage and keep us accountable don't happen overnight—we have to be there through the ups and downs of life together.

18. What friendship has had the greatest positive impact on your life?

Why has that relationship been so special?

How can you incorporate that element into your other core friendships?

Jesus had a purpose in investing in the 72 and the Twelve—He was preparing them to continue the ministry that He had started. Our friendships have purpose as well.

Dear Father, thank You for sending Your Son, Jesus, to be the ultimate example in every area of life. I also thank You for the gift of friendship. Help me to be a good steward of the relationships with which You have blessed me, as I learn to invest my time and energy in the right places. Teach me to be deeper with few rather than shallow with many—including my relationship with You. Amen.

Note

1. This story is a fictional account. Any resemblance to actual events or people, living or dead, is purely coincidental.

REACHING *Out*

ENCOURAGING OTHERS

Therefore encourage one another and build each other up,
just as in fact you are doing. And we urge you, brothers, warn those who
are idle, encourage the timid, help the weak, be patient with everyone.

1 THESSALONIANS 5:11,14

EVERYDAY WOMAN

"This is the worst day of my life," Lynn mumbled as she left her manager's office. It didn't matter that every day since she started her new job seemed to be worse than the last. Though 47 years old, she felt like a child who had been reprimanded by the principal whenever she had to meet with her manager. Despite the mist that filled her eyes, she managed to find the front door of the building. Once outside the tears spilled down her cheeks.

Lynn tried to stop short of sobbing, but it was no use. *This isn't worth it, God!* she thought. *Surely the boys can find another way to get through college. I don't know how much more of this I can take. Nothing I do is ever good enough for this company!* After walking a few laps around the parking lot, Lynn regained her composure. She blotted the mascara that was dripping from her eyes with a tissue as she made her way back inside and plopped into the chair at her desk.

The delicate purple orchid next to her computer immediately caught her attention. It was a beautiful single flower, set carefully atop a blue sticky note. "Lynn—thought you could use some beauty today. I'm praying for you." The note wasn't signed, but there was only one person in the building who had orchids on her desk, and that person was the only coworker Lynn knew who shared her belief in prayer.

Thank you, Sharon. You have no idea how much I need this right now. As Lynn gazed at the exquisitely delicate petals, a hopeful smile tugged at the corners of her mouth. *Thank You, Lord. Thank You for Sharon and her thoughtfulness today.*[1]

Each of us has experienced timely encouragement from someone that made the difference between sinking and swimming. "A word aptly spoken is like apples of gold in settings of silver" (Proverbs 25:11). Whether spoken, written or acted out, encouragement is one of the greatest blessings we can offer our friends; and the best part is, unlike 18-karat apples, it doesn't cost us a thing!

1. Describe a time when a friend's encouragement blessed you. What did she do? How did it make you feel?

2. Describe the most recent thing you did to encourage a friend. What was your friend's response?

3. Write your own proverb about encouragement. (Browse through the book of Proverbs if you need inspiration.)

One of the treasures of friendships is the encouragement we can offer one another in times of need.

ETERNAL WISDOM

Let's look at the two most common Greek words that convey the idea of encouragement. The first, *paraklesis*, means "a calling to one's side," and is translated "consolation" or "comfort" 20 of the 29 times the word is used in the *King James Version* of the New Testament.[2] The second, *parakaleo*, similarly means "to call to one's side or to one's aid."[3]

In the *New American Standard Bible*, "paraklesis" and "parakaleo" are used 10 times in 2 Corinthians 1:3-7 (all translated "comfort"). Read this passage and then answer the following questions:

4. Why does God comfort us in our troubles (v. 4)?

What does His comfort produce (v. 6)?

Why is it important to comfort and encourage those who are suffering?

The Encourager

Because our Father is the "God of all comfort" (2 Corinthians 1:3), He showed His suffering children compassion by promising us someone who would be our advocate and comforter; someone who would come to our side when we need help—a parakletos.[4]

5. Read the following passages. Who is our parakletos and what does each passage have to say about the role He plays in our lives?

    John 14:16,26

    John 15:26

    John 16:7

6. According to Acts 9:31, what role does the Holy Spirit play?

It's interesting to note that the word "encouraged" in Acts 9:31 is a word we looked at earlier: "paraklesis." So what's the connection? Let's take a look.

Our Role as Encouragers

As we saw earlier, God sent the Holy Spirit to be our parakletos—our comforter, teacher and encourager; someone to come to our side when we need Him. In a nutshell, God sent the Holy Spirit to be a paraklesis—to console, comfort and encourage.

Now here's the exciting part! God calls us to be a part of the Holy Spirit's work, though on a much smaller scale.

7. According to 1 Thessalonians 5:11,14, how are we commanded to encourage others?

What is the purpose of such encouragement, as found in Hebrews 3:12-13?

We are called to be little comforters—encouragers with a lowercase *e*—little *parakletoi* (the plural form of "parakletos"), if you will. Our encouragement may take many forms, but whether we are exhorting others to live rightly (see 1 Timothy 4:13, *NKJV*), teaching from Scripture (see Romans 15:4), comforting the discouraged (see 1 Thessalonians 5:11) or urging others to serve God (see Romans 12:1), we are taking part in paraklesis.

8. In which of these forms of encouragement—exhorting, teaching, comforting or urging—are you most gifted?

In what other ways can you offer encouragement (e.g., being a good listener, being thoughtful)?

As members of the Body of Christ, we have a special responsibility to encourage our brothers and sisters in the Lord. How much more then should we seek ways to encourage, comfort and exhort our closest friends?

9. List some practical ways we can encourage our friends.

Did your answer include the simplest yet most effective form of encouragement: apt words? The written or spoken word is incredibly powerful. What comes out of your mouth has the power to either break others down or send them floating on cloud nine. "The tongue has the power of life and death" (Proverbs 18:21).

Contrary to popular belief, becoming close with a friend does not give you license to become too casual with your words. As Oliver Wendell Holmes, Jr., said,

> Don't flatter yourself that friendship authorizes you to say disagreeable things to your intimates. The nearer you come into relation with a person, the more necessary do tact and courtesy become.[5]

10. Why do you think that some people tear others down with sarcastic or cutting remarks even though they are friends?

11. What admonition regarding our words is found in Matthew 12:34?

12. According to Ephesians 4:29, what should be coming out of our mouths?

13. List your closest friends in the following chart; then write down something you could say to each friend (either in person or in writing) that would build her up according to her needs (see Ephesians 4:29).

Friend	Words of Encouragement

Like Lynn, our Everyday Woman, there's no doubt you've benefited from a friend's thoughtfulness at one time or another. Although there are many ways to encourage others, our creative genius seems to dry up just when we need a good idea, doesn't it? Let's brainstorm some practical ways to encourage your friends so that you'll always have a resource when you need a good idea, fast! Since most women are encouraged in similar ways, finding those things that tickle your fancy will help you do the same for others.

14. On what special occasions would you like to be remembered by others?

15. How do you like to receive encouragement (e.g., notes, thoughtful gifts, spontaneous phone calls)?

16. What are some of the most encouraging things others have done for you?

Complete the following chart using your answers from questions 14 through 16 along with the things you already know about your friends. During the upcoming week, accumulate as much information for the chart as possible from your friends and come up with at least three ideas for encouraging each friend.

Name	Birthday	Special Occasions	Favorites (Color, Hobby, Flower, Fragrance, Etc.)	Ideas for Encouragement
				1. 2. 3.
				1. 2. 3.
				1. 2. 3.
				1. 2. 3.
				1. 2. 3.
				1. 2. 3.

Before you complete the last session in this study, bless each friend listed by implementing at least one of the ideas. Note the date you completed it.

Notes

1. This story is a fictional account. Any resemblance to actual events or people, living or dead, is purely coincidental.
2. James Strong, *The New Strong's Exhaustive Concordance of the Bible* (Nashville, TN: Thomas Nelson Publishers, 2001), #3874.
3. Ibid., #3870.
4. Ibid., #3875.
5. Bob Phillips, *Phillips' Awesome Collection of Quips and Quotes* (Eugene, OR: Harvest House Publishers, 2001), p. 171.

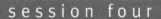
READY TO
Reveal
BEING HONEST AND VULNERABLE

But he said to me, "My grace is sufficient for you, for my power is made perfect in
weakness." Therefore I will boast all the more gladly about my weaknesses, so that Christ's
power may rest on me. That is why, for Christ's sake, I delight in weaknesses, in insults,
in hardships, in persecutions, in difficulties. For when I am weak, then I am strong.
2 CORINTHIANS 12:9-10

Every man, however wise, needs the advice of some sagacious friend in the affairs of life.
TITUS MACCIUS PLAUTUS

EVERYDAY WOMAN

"Joy, I need to talk to you about something." Allison's voice cracked slightly
as she said the words.

"Sure, Ali, what's up?" Joy knew there was something terribly wrong.
During the 15 years since they had met and had become best friends, she had
only seen Allison this upset one time—when Allison's husband left after four
years of marriage. In fact, Allison never showed much emotion at all—she
always seemed to have the ability to bounce back and keep going. Joy was
usually the one to bare her soul or ask Allison for advice, not the other way
around.

"It's about Justin and me."

Now Joy was really concerned. Thoughts swirled in her mind. *Dear God, please don't let it be that he's broken up with her! They're so perfect for each other, and they're such an example of purity—they've waited so long for You to bring the right person into their lives, and now they finally have each other. Their commitment to remain pure in their relationship is such a testament to You! I thought for sure Justin would ask her to marry him any day now. What is it, Lord? I've never seen Ali like this, and I don't know what to do.*

Allison saw the confused look on Joy's face, so she forced out the words, "Joy," she began as she took a deep breath, "I'm pregnant."

Joy's stomach jumped through her throat. It seemed like eternity passed before she could muster the courage to ask, "Allison, what happened? You said you two were doing so well avoiding situations that could lead to that!"

"I know," Allison said, "but I just didn't know how to tell you what was really going on. It's so stupid, but I thought it would do more harm than good; I thought it was better that you didn't know. It just sort of happened the first time, and then I was so embarrassed to tell anyone—and Justin and I kept telling each other that we were going to stop." The tears flowed freely as Allison said, "I can't believe I was so stupid, Joy! I'm so sorry I lied to you."

Joy wrapped her arms around Allison and cried with her. Her heart broke, but not for herself. "Ali, you know I still love you and I'm going to be here for you no matter what. I just wish you would have told me sooner, so I could've *helped* you."[1]

Our culture screams, "Be your own person! What you do is no one else's business!" We are encouraged to make it to the top at all costs and to fill our schedules with me-me-me activities. Satan also does everything in his power to make us believe that we are alone and that the things we struggle against are unique or even shameful.

The individualistic air we breathe in our present society is foreign to many parts of the world. Most cultures—including the Middle Eastern culture in which the Scriptures were written—are more community minded than our culture. Perhaps that's why it is so easy for us to ignore the many admonitions in Scripture for us to bear one another's burdens, to be honest with others about the state of our heart and to confess our sins to each other (see Galatians 6:2, Ephesians 4:25 and James 5:16).

1. What do you think breeds individuality in our culture?

2. What are the dangers of being so individualistic that you don't confide in anyone?

Ironically, many women feel that their friendships are too superficial—not because their friendships aren't real, but because they aren't deep. Ladies, if we want to go deeper, we have to be willing to pay the cost: emotional honesty. Are you willing to bear your soul, even if it means you don't look like you have it all together?

ETERNAL WISDOM

Before you answer the previous question, let's take a look at some facts concerning vulnerability.

- **Fact Number One:** We only venture past superficiality when we decide the benefits of a relationship are worth the risk of potential hurt, judgment, jealousy, discouragement and rejection.
- **Fact Number Two:** When we embrace our worth in Christ, we are free to take the risks involved in relationships because we know that our weaknesses are not something we should fear.

The apostle Paul understood the importance of being honest about his weaknesses.

To keep me from becoming conceited . . . there was given me a thorn in my flesh, a messenger of Satan, to torment me. Three times I pleaded with the Lord to take it away from me. But he said to me, "My grace is sufficient for you, for my power is made perfect [*teleioo*] in weakness." Therefore I will boast [*kauchaomai*] all the more gladly about my weaknesses, so that Christ's power may rest on me. That is why, for Christ's sake, I delight in weaknesses, in insults, in hardships, in persecutions, in difficulties. For when I am weak [*astheneo*], then I am strong [*dunatos*] (2 Corinthians 12:7-10, original Greek words added).

Let's take a closer look at this passage.

3. From what sinful attitude was God protecting Paul by giving him a "thorn in [the] flesh"?

Do you think that the thorn would have helped Paul overcome this sinful attitude if he had decided not to tell anyone about it? Why or why not?

The trials, hardships and difficulties we face in life serve to keep us humble. When we hide those struggles from others, we actually fight against God's discipline and prevent ourselves from receiving healing.

4. How is putting up a false front a symptom of pride?

What types of struggles in your life are you most inclined to hide from others? Why?

Paul asked God to take his infirmity away, but God replied that His grace was sufficient for Paul, for His "power is made perfect in weakness" (v. 9). The Greek verb translated "made perfect" is "teleioo," which means to complete, to accomplish or (figuratively) to consummate.[2]

5. How do your weaknesses complete God's power?

Quite a paradox, isn't it? The more weaknesses we have, the more opportunities we have to glorify God through them. The catch? We have to be willing to lay our pride aside to let God work through those things we'd rather hide.

Paul was willing to accept that challenge. In fact, he said that rather than mitigate his damages, he would *boast* in his weaknesses! The Greek word translated "boast" is "kauchaomai," which is akin to the word "vaunt."[3]

6. Look up the word "vaunt" in a dictionary and write out the definition.

What ironic statement was Paul making in his choice of the word "boast" or "vaunt"?

God is glorified through our weaknesses in several ways. His power is perfected through our difficulties as we draw our strength from Him and remain dependent on His grace. He is also glorified as we share with others how He has sustained us and has helped us grow spiritually. Matthew Henry wrote, "When God's people communicate their experiences, let them always remember to take notice of what God has done to keep them humble, as well as what he has done in favor to them and for their advancement."[4] It is good to share with others how God has blessed you emotionally, materially and spiritually, but you can't stop there! You also have to share how God has been refining and testing you and how you've responded to such challenges.

7. How can God be glorified when you are honest about your weaknesses with others?

8. How might others benefit from your honesty?

   How might you benefit?

9. Second Corinthians 12:10 says, "For when I am weak, then I am strong." Using the following definitions and the material we've already discussed, explain this paradox.

   - Weak (astheneo)—"to be weak, feeble, to be without strength, powerless"[5]
   - Strong (dunatos)—"powerful or capable"[6]

God always blesses us when we choose to glorify Him. When we bring Him glory by being vulnerable with others, what benefits will we reap? The answer is obvious—but what exactly does being vulnerable mean?

ENDURING HOPE

To define vulnerability in friendship, let's turn to an unlikely source—a game called Contract Bridge. You don't have to be familiar with the game to understand the concept. To be vulnerable in a game of Bridge means that you are "liable to increased penalties but entitled to increased bonuses after winning a game."[7] Simply put, there are risks, but the benefits are far more enticing if you're playing to win!

To further define vulnerability, examine the following chart:

Vulnerability Is	Vulnerability Is Not
• Letting go of your pride and letting others see your struggles	• Doing everything possible to look like you have it all together
• Confessing your sins to others so that you can receive healing	• Revealing another's shortcomings or putting him or her down in front of others
• Asking advice from those you trust and accepting their help	• Dumping your cares on others without being sensitive to their needs
• Asking for prayer through difficult seasons	• Gossiping about others or sharing others' faults with your friends
• Being accountable to your core group of friends	• Sharing the deepest part of you with *everyone* you talk to
• Being honest about your feelings, frustrations and needs	• Being insensitive to or insulting others when they displease you
• Being confident in God's grace so that you can rejoice in your weaknesses	• Being insecure or always focusing on your weaknesses—false humility
• Realizing that your struggles are not unique; you are not alone	• Isolating yourself from accountability for fear of rejection and shame
• Encouraging/teaching others through the difficulties you face	• Griping to others about your hardships

10. In which areas of being vulnerable are you strongest?

On which areas do you need to work?

11. What do the following verses teach us about vulnerability in friendship?

Proverbs 16:18

Ephesians 4:25

James 5:16

12. Based on all we've studied about vulnerability, what advice would you have given Allison, our Everyday Woman, on the subject?

EVERYDAY LIFE

Vulnerability in friendships is one of those topics that is very easy to study and affirm on paper but is extremely difficult for most of us to put into practice. Our pride—our fear of being hurt or rejected and our belief that a good

Christian shouldn't struggle—keep most of us trapped in a cage of isolation. Satan would love to keep us crippled and hiding, but God calls us to something much greater: solidarity among the Body of Christ that stems from mutual vulnerability.

Before you answer the following questions, spend some time asking God to search your heart and to prepare you to be honest with yourself and with Him.

13. In what ways have you been hiding hurts, struggles, temptations, questions or fears?

With whom do you specifically need to share these struggles?

14. Look over the items listed in the Vulnerability Is Not section of the chart. In what ways have you abused or taken advantage of your friends?

What practical steps can you take to become more vulnerable with your friends?

Our emotional and spiritual health depends more on our vulnerability with God than with anyone else. As this session comes to a close, bare your soul before Him. You can pray the following prayer, or if you prefer, you may write your own prayer.

> *Dear Father, thank You for being glorified in my weaknesses. May I boast in them because I am confident that Your strength shows up best in my weak places. Teach me to lay down my pride so that I can be more vulnerable with the friends with whom You have blessed me. Most of all, make me more like Your Son, Jesus Christ, who humbled Himself to the point of death—the ultimate model of vulnerability. It's in His precious name I pray. Amen.*

Notes

1. This story is a fictional account. Any resemblance to actual events or people, living or dead, is purely coincidental.
2. James Strong, *The New Strong's Exhaustive Concordance of the Bible* (Nashville, TN: Thomas Nelson Publishers, 2001), Greek #5048.
3. Ibid., Greek #2744.
4. Matthew Henry, "Commentary on 2 Corinthians." *Matthew Henry Concise Commentary on the Whole Bible*, version 7.0.5, e-Sword.
5. Strong, *The New Strong's Exhaustive Concordance*, Greek #770.
6. Ibid., Greek #1415.
7. *Merriam-Webster's Collegiate Dictionary*, 11th ed., s.v. "vulnerable."

RING! RING!
Anyone Home?
THE FINE ART OF LISTENING

He who answers before listening—that is his folly and his shame.
PROVERBS 18:13

*My dear brothers, take note of this: Everyone should be
quick to listen, slow to speak and slow to become angry.*
JAMES 1:19

EVERYDAY WOMAN

Jai moaned as traffic came to a halt. Though she loved her suburban life, the traffic from her job in the city to her home in suburbia was more than she could bear sometimes. Red taillights trailed into the distance as far as she could see. *Just a couple more weeks until my transfer, and then I'll never have to deal with this traffic again!* Suddenly Jai couldn't wait to get out of the city. She turned up the radio and tried to forget where she was, mulling over the day's events as her car inched slowly along the freeway.

Tuesdays were usually one of Jai's favorite days, but not this one. Her weekly Tuesday lunches with Megan were times to get away from the office to laugh together and catch up on—*to catch up on Megan's life*, Jai realized. She had never cared before today that Megan usually did most of the talking. *I'm such an introvert; besides, I never have anything exciting to share. Megan always tells the funniest stories, and her life is so much more exciting than mine. Why would I bore her with my life's details?* she thought. But today Jai had wanted to share the news of her transfer to another state, and she couldn't seem to find a good opportunity to do so. *I know that Megan cares about me and that she would want to know, but the way she talks about her life all the time makes it seem like she's not interested in me.*[1]

⚬

Our schools may offer courses in public speaking, but whatever happened to the fine art of listening? Listening to others is a vital part of every relationship—especially friendships. Howard G. Hendricks made the following observation:

> It's easy to teach people how to speak. It's very difficult to teach them how to listen. And by the way, have you looked in the mirror lately? Did you notice you have two ears but only one mouth? Imagine if God had reversed that.[2]

Although the mental picture of someone with two mouths and one ear is rather humorous, the implications are not. How often do we act as if we were not only bigmouthed but also *bimouthed*? Take a deep breath and get ready for an honest look at yourself!

1. During your conversations with others, what percentage of time do you spend listening? (Circle your answer, and *be honest with yourself!*)

 0   10   20   30   40   50   60   70   80   90   100

The truth is, listening well is a timeless art form, and most of us could use a lesson in it. Let's look a little closer at what it means to truly listen.

ETERNAL WISDOM

Words are necessary for communication; our speech communicates feelings, needs and observations. Did you know, however, that listening also communicates, albeit more subtly. The book of James is full of admonitions concerning both our speaking and listening abilities.

2. What admonition is found in James 1:19?

In context, this verse primarily refers to our ability to listen to the Word of God. However, many commentators agree that the principle of being more ready to listen than to speak applies to every area of our life.

3. Throughout the ages, scholars have echoed James 1:19. Give an example how each of the following phrases could be applied to your speech (or lack thereof!):

"The ears are always open, ever ready to receive instruction; but the tongue is surrounded with a double row of teeth, to hedge it in, and to keep it within proper bounds."[3]

"Be swift to hear, and with deep consideration give answer."[4]

"Men have two ears, and but one tongue, that they should hear more than they speak."[5]

"I have sometimes had occasion to regret that I have spoken, never that I was silent."[6]

"[Silence] is the spice of speech, and the chief of all spices."[7]

4. What do the following verses teach us about speaking with discernment?

Proverbs 10:19

Proverbs 13:3

Proverbs 15:2

Ecclesiastes 5:2

Listening to others does not mean passively taking in everything we hear. For example, being a good listener does not mean you must entertain idle or unprofitable talk, gossip, inappropriate language or topics, dirty jokes or blasphemy. It does mean that you should listen attentively to wholesome advice, good instructions, the experiences of others and, above all, the teaching of the Word of God.

Let's take a look at the components of effective listening, as found in Proverbs 18:13: "He who answers before listening—that is his folly and his shame."

Hear

The first component of listening is physically hearing what the other person is saying. This involves minimizing other distractions that might cause us to miss pertinent information. It also includes making eye contact with the person talking so that we can observe her body language as well as hear her words.

5. List some practical ways to ensure that we hear all the pertinent information being conveyed and ways that convey that we are listening intently.

Consider

The Hebrew word *shama* translated as "listening" in Proverbs 18:13, "He who answers before listening—that is his folly and his shame" denotes more than just hearing with our ears. Depending on the context, it also can mean "to gain or get knowledge," "to agree with [the message's] petition or intent" and "to give undivided attention."[8] Moses used the word "shama" when he told Israel's judges to hear the cases of the people (see Deuteronomy 1:16). Moses meant that they should do more than listen to the words; he meant that they should consider the merits of the case so that they could render a just decision. "Shama" is also used in Deuteronomy 6:4, "Hear [shama], O Israel: The LORD our God, the LORD is one." Moses then gave several vital commands to the Israelites that he wanted them to internalize.

6. Based on the definition of "shama," list some things we should consider when we listen to others.

Respond

A response should only come after careful consideration and only if a response is appropriate. Answering before we have heard and considered what the other person said is foolish and will only bring us shame. We must choose our timing carefully and refrain from responding until we are sure the other person has finished speaking. Before responding, we should ask ourselves several questions.

- *Is this person looking for advice, or does she simply need a listening ear? If she needs just a listening ear, what can I say to let her know I am here for her?*
- *Is my response based on my own experiences or on God's Word?*
- *Will my response help her, or am I simply looking for a way to share my own similar experience?*
- *Is my response clothed with grace and humility?*
- *Does my response show that I care about this person?*

ENDURING HOPE

There are times when a verbal response is neither necessary nor appropriate. This is usually true when a friend or loved one is expressing pain or grief. In those delicate moments, calculated silence can do far more good than a host of well-meaning words.

The book of Job is an excellent textbook for learning how to respond to those who are mourning or expressing grief.

7. In Job 2:11-13, how did Job's friends initially respond to his agony?

Job's friends came to his side for the Jewish practice of mourning, called *sheva*. For seven days they sat with Job without saying a word. They wept with him, mourned his losses and listened while he lamented the day he was born. Those seven days of silence were the best thing those friends could offer Job.

8. What was Eliphaz's first mistake, as suggested by Job 4:2?

Days of dialogue ensued. All but one of Job's friends tried to give their own explanation for Job's miserable state, which only increased his agony. Although each meant well, they had no way of knowing the heavenly plan that was taking place. Their words and speculations only made Job feel worse.

9. According to Job 16:2-5, how did Job respond to the words of his friends?

What advice did he give on how to comfort others?

10. Think of a time when you have been overcome by grief. What was the best thing a friend did or could have done for you in that moment?

The fine art of listening and the discipline of silence are never more valuable than when comforting a hurting individual. If there is such a friend in your life now, take a few moments to think of ways you can purposefully implement these two practices. Write your ideas in the space provided.

EVERYDAY LIFE

One of the best ways to evaluate and maintain your listening skills is the 2-Q test. The 2-Q test works as follows: When conversing with someone, respond to each topic with at least two questions. Asking questions in response to a person's statements communicates that you have heard what the person said, that you have considered what you heard and that you are interested in what that person has to say.

Let's look at Jai, our Everyday Woman, as an example. If Megan had implemented the 2-Q test at lunch that Tuesday, their conversation might have gone something like this:

> Jai: I got some news at work this week. I've accepted a transfer to our newest office just outside Reno, Nevada.
> Megan: You're kidding! Why do you want to move? (Question 1)
> Jai: Well, I've been thinking for quite a while now that it might be nice to get out of the city, but I hadn't been actively pursuing it. I didn't think it would become a reality, so I never mentioned it to you.
> Megan: So how did you come to this decision? (Question 2)
> Jai: Actually, my boss approached me with the idea. She said I was the best person she could think of to train the team at our new facility.
> Megan: What an honor! I'm so excited for you, Jai! Oh, but I will miss you so much!
> Jai: I know! That will be the hardest part about moving: leaving you behind. But we must keep in touch, and you can come visit me often!

11. Now it's time to put the 2-Q test to work. For each of the following statements that a friend could say to you, write two questions that you could ask in response:

"I've been really swamped at work (or at home)."

"My daughter just had her first baby."

"My husband seems really tired and run down lately."

"I just got back from a great weekend getaway."

Make the 2-Q test a game this week. You may feel silly, especially if you're not used to responding to others with questions, but the person who is speaking won't mind your interest. She *will* notice your attentiveness, even if she doesn't verbalize her gratitude.

As you learn to honor your friends by offering them your listening ear, you might be surprised to discover that it's contagious. Eventually others will catch on and will start showing you the same consideration. Implementing the fine art of listening will help turn your more superficial relationships into ones with deeper meaning and more blessings.

Notes

1. This story is a fictional account. Any resemblance to actual events or people, living or dead, is purely coincidental.
2. Howard G. Hendricks, "Prayer: The Christian's Secret Weapon," *Veritas*, vol. 4, no. 1 (January, 2004).
3. Albert Barnes, "Commentary on James 1:19," *Albert Barnes' Notes on the Bible*, version 7.0.5, e-Sword.
4. Ibid.
5. Ibid.
6. Ibid.
7. Jewish saying, quoted in John Gill, "Commentary on James 1:19," *John Gill's Exposition of the Entire Bible*, version 7.0.5, e-Sword.
8. James Strong, *The New Strong's Exhaustive Concordance of the Bible* (Nashville, TN: Thomas Nelson Publishers, 2001), Hebrew #8085.

Receiving AND *Giving* CORRECTION

CLOTHED IN GRACE AND HUMILITY

> *Whoever turns a sinner from the error of his way will*
> *save him from death and cover over a multitude of sins.*
>
> JAMES 5:20

> *My son, do not make light of the Lord's discipline, and do not lose heart when he rebukes you,*
> *because the Lord disciplines those he loves, and he punishes everyone he accepts as a son.*
>
> HEBREWS 12:5-6

E V E R Y D A Y   W O M A N

Adrianne felt her face turn red as anger swelled within her. She tried to keep from raising her voice, but it was no use. "I can take everyone else judging me, but not you, Laura—not my best friend!" she shouted.

Laura felt the sting of tears forming in her eyes and the lump in her throat grew more unbearable each second. She hadn't meant to hurt Adrianne, but for weeks she had felt the Lord urging her to confront her friend about her attitude toward her husband.

"Adrianne, I'm not judging you. I care about you, and I care about your marriage, which is why I brought it up in the first place. I've been around you two since you started dating, and something has changed lately. Your anger toward Craig is beginning to hurt your relationship, and I'm worried about you. And to be completely honest, Adrianne," Laura tried to choose her words carefully, "it's becoming harder as your friend to be around you these days because you're always complaining about Craig. It seems like you don't want to find anything positive to talk about anymore. I love you, Adrianne, and I want you to experience the joy of a healthy marriage."

"You're just like everybody else, Laura. You don't know the whole story, yet you pretend to have all the answers. It makes me sick! Do you want to be my judge or my friend? You can't be both." Adrianne's gaze dropped to the floor as she said the words. She thought, *That sounds harsh, but it's true! Why can't everyone just let me live my life? It's not like they don't have dirty laundry too! Besides, the Bible says you're not supposed to judge others.*

Laura was speechless. She tried frantically to think of a way to get out of there as quickly as possible, but she knew it would be wrong to run away at this crucial moment. *Should I apologize? Should I be more firm? Is this worth losing our friendship over? Lord, please help me!*[1]

Most of us at one time or another have had to confront someone else about something unpleasant. And often, no matter how carefully we present it, there are hurt feelings or even angry rebuttals. We hope that the other person will eventually see the truth in what we say.

1. Briefly describe a time when you had to give constructive criticism to someone (without naming names). What was the other person's initial reaction? Did the person eventually accept the correction?

    What did you learn from the experience?

2. What is your usual response when a friend or family member offers correction to you?

Is there a difference between how you respond to a friend and how you respond to a relative? Why?

It is a fact of life that you will be the giver of correction as well as the recipient at various times during your lifetime. Let's discover some important aspects of the give and take of constructive criticism.

ETERNAL WISDOM

Judging Others

Ask most people what the Bible has to say about judging others and even nonbelievers will give a rough quote of Matthew 7:1: "Do not judge, or you too will be judged." While ignoring the rest of Scripture, society has deemed this verse all-encompassing and doesn't hesitate to use the "don't judge me" defense whenever threatened by disapproval of any kind.

Elisabeth Elliot noted the problem with the following line of reasoning:

> The current popular notion that judging others is in itself a sin leads to such inappropriate maxims as "I'm OK and you're OK." It encourages a conspiracy of moral indifference which says, "If you never tell me that anything I'm doing is wrong, I'll never tell you that anything you're doing is wrong."
>
> "Judge not that ye be not judged" has come to mean that if you never call anything sin, nobody can ever call you a sinner. You do your thing and let me do mine and let's accept everybody and never mind what they're up to.[2]

3. What does 1 Corinthians 5:12-13 tell us about judging nonbelievers and believers? Why do you think there is a distinction between judging nonbelievers and judging believers?

It might be helpful to clarify what it means to judge. *Merriam-Webster's Collegiate Dictionary* defines "judge" as, "to form an opinion about through careful weighing of evidence and testing of premises."[3] "Careful weighing of evidence" is the operative phrase.

4. How would you test a premise?

Weighing a person's actions is for the purpose of recognizing when godly correction is in order (i.e., when their actions contradict biblical principles). We must never judge others for selfish reasons (e.g., jealousy, gossip, pride), and we should temper every judgment with the recognition of the incredible amount of grace we've been extended by God.

5. According to James 5:19-20, what is the ultimate goal of godly correction?

How might Matthew 7:1-4 help us check our motives for judging others?

Now that we have a better understanding of judging, let's take a closer look at correction.

Correction

Receiving and giving correction are both vital to our growth as Christians. Our attitude toward these two disciplines influences our spiritual growth. How we view correction, how we respond to correction and how we give correction are three areas that help to reveal our commitment to becoming closer to Christ and more like Him. Our natural tendency in response to correction is to view it as hurtful, unnecessary, unfair, judgmental or as a personal attack. Let's face it, we have all dealt with these reactions at one time or another.

6. According to Hebrews 12:5-11, how should we view the Lord's discipline?

   How might God discipline us through another's correction?

7. What insight does Proverbs 27:5 give us about how to view correction from others?

Responding to Correction
Our view of correction will in part dictate our reaction to it. Our heart can only travel where our head leads. In other words, having a clear understanding of correction will cause our emotions to fall in line. But whether or not we *feel* good about it, heeding correction is nonnegotiable.

8. Proverbs is full of admonitions about how we are to respond to correction. Read the following verses, and then summarize the main point of each verse:

Proverbs 10:17

Proverbs 15:31

Proverbs 19:20

"Listen," "accept," "wise"—are you seeing a trend? However wrong we think others may be in their view of us or our actions, we are commanded to listen with patient ears and an open, humble heart, remembering that one of God's most frequent modes of discipline is correction from others.

9. Sometimes you may receive from someone you trust a rebuke that is completely off base. What is the best course of action in such a situation?

You can choose to respond to correction with indignation, anger, self-pity or defensiveness, or you can choose to respond with humility, prayer, grace, thankfulness and a resolve to change when it is appropriate to do so. The choice is yours.

Giving Correction

As Laura, our Everyday Woman, learned, giving correction can be one of the hardest things we ever have to do. Just as loving parents lament having to discipline their beloved child, so we grieve over having to tell a friend something that is probably going to hurt her.

10. According to Proverbs 28:23, what hope is there for people giving correction?

God has not left us to our own devices to figure out how to confront others; instead He has given us specific guidelines.

11. Fill in the following blanks using Matthew 18:15-17.

The purpose of confrontation is to reveal the other person's _____.

Initially confront the person _____. If that doesn't work, take _____ or _____ others to act as witnesses.

If the person still refuses to listen, take it to _____.

If the person still does not listen, treat the person as you would an _____.

Before you confront any believer, consider the following four steps to confrontation:

Step One—Ask
- What is the heart of the matter? Is it a sin issue or a matter of spiritual liberty (see 1 Corinthians 10:29)?
- What is the best way to approach the subject?
- Am I the best person to confront this person? (Do not let this question turn into an excuse for passivity!)
- What are my motives? Are they pure?
- Should I seek counsel before I confront this person? If so, to whom should I go? (He or she should be a fellow believer who

would be objective—don't use it as an opportunity to gossip.)

Step Two—Pray
- Ask God for wisdom and discernment.
- Seek God's heart to make sure your motives are pure.
- Ask God for the appropriate time and place according to His will.
- Ask God to prepare the other person's heart.

Step Three—Confront
- "Restore him [or her] gently" (Galatians 6:1).
- Demonstrate understanding and empathy.
- Use appropriate Scriptures.
- Clothe yourself in humility.
- Speak clearly and calmly.

Step Four—Follow Up
- Don't abandon the person after you've confronted her. Instead, restore her to the best of your ability (see Matthew 18:17 for those who refuse to heed correction).
- Offer to meet and pray with her as she grows in the area you've addressed.
- Demonstrate your genuine desire to help the person you've confronted by not acting differently toward her afterward.

Following these guidelines for giving correction will help minimize the other person's defensiveness toward the correction. This method does not guarantee the rebuke will be effective—that part is up to the individual you're confronting—but it will eliminate any reason to blame yourself for any fallout.

ENDURING HOPE

Have you ever looked into a magnifying mirror? You know, the ones that magnify every tiny blemish? Some people refuse to own one, clinging to the false hope that if they don't know those blemishes are there, the blemishes can't exist!

Relationships are God's favorite magnifying mirror. Our friendships magnify our every fault, revealing to others who we truly are. The closer we get to someone, the more glaring our faults (and theirs!) become. We can refuse to look in the mirror, but that doesn't mean that what we refuse to see does not exist. In fact, as painful as it can be, looking in the mirror of friendships will help us discover the ugliest blemishes so that we can address them.

12. What are some of the blemishes you have discovered about yourself as your relationships have deepened?

How do you try to cover up these blemishes (e.g., ignore them, convince yourself they're not *that* bad, blame others)?

Pride is one of the biggest hindrances to spiritual growth. Unfortunately, it's also a hard habit to kick. In God's sovereignty, He has given relationships to us so that we can focus not on ourselves, but on others. We need to listen to those God has placed in our lives—they are often the mouthpiece He uses to catch our stubborn attention!

13. List the people whom you feel God placed in your life as your magnifying mirror.

How does your attitude toward godly correction given by those people need to change?

Take a moment to think of a scenario where confrontation would be necessary. It could be a situation you are currently facing, one you have faced in the past, one you have made up or one based on our Everyday Woman story. Divide a sheet of paper into four columns and then label the columns as follows: "Ask," "Pray," "Confront" and "Follow Up." Using the guidelines we discussed in the "Giving Correction" section, fill in the chart specific to your scenario. The activity will be more powerful if you actually apply it to your life, so take it seriously.

Make time this week to pray the following prayer often:

> *Gracious Father, thank You for loving me enough to discipline me. Open my eyes to those things You would teach me through the correction of others. Help me lay my pride aside and prayerfully consider any truth in their rebukes so that I can grow in wisdom. Lord, clothe my tongue in grace and humility when I have occasion to confront my sisters in Christ. Search out and purge any impure motive from my heart. I pray these things in Christ's precious name. Amen.*

Notes

1. This story is a fictional account. Any resemblance to actual events or people, living or dead, is purely coincidental.
2. Elisabeth Elliot, *On Asking God Why* (Old Tappan, NJ: F. H. Revell, 1989), n.p.
3. *Merriam-Webster's Collegiate Dictionary*, 11th ed., s.v. "judge."

Redeeming THE WRECKAGE

FORGIVENESS

Bear with each other and forgive whatever grievances you may have against one another. Forgive as the Lord forgave you.

COLOSSIANS 3:13

I firmly believe that a great many prayers are not answered because we are not willing to forgive someone.

DWIGHT L. MOODY

EVERYDAY WOMAN

"All right, ladies, for this section we're going to divide into pairs to pray for one another," the small-group leader announced. Suddenly the room erupted with chatter as the women picked partners. After everyone settled down, the leader noticed that there were two women left alone. "Nicole and Erin, why don't you two pair up?" she suggested.

Nicole froze in a moment of panic. *Out of all the women here, how did I get stuck with Erin?* she thought. She watched in horror as her former friend gathered her things, picked up her chair and walked toward her. Nicole's mind was drowning in a sea of noisy thoughts. *I can't pray for her, God. Not after the way she betrayed my confidence. Being cordial to her is one thing; I've even stayed in this Bible study, though I wanted to get out—but praying for her? That's just more than I'm ready for.*

When Nicole discovered that Erin had shared some sensitive, personal information about her with mutual friends of theirs, the wound had cut deep. Now as she watched Erin prepare to cross the room, the wound became raw and painful again. *What am I going to do?* Nicole pleaded with God. *It's not like I can say, "I'm sorry Erin, why don't you ask someone else to pray for you?" Everyone would think I'm the worst person in the world! Look at her—she's walking over here like nothing ever happened! I've got to think fast!*

Before Nicole could say or do anything about her predicament, Erin was positioning her chair next to her former friend's. *O God,* Nicole silently prayed. *Help me get through this! I can't even look her in the face, let alone pray for her!*[1]

When we invest our time and emotions into a relationship, allowing ourselves to trust and be vulnerable with others, there are bound to be times when we get hurt. We are imperfect, sinful creatures, and none of us is immune to hurting others or being hurt ourselves. The truth is, no matter how strong our friendship bonds are, without forgiveness every single one of our friendships would be short lived!

Forgiveness can be tricky. It is intangible, and as such, it can be difficult to know if you've truly forgiven someone. Can you relate to any of the following statements?

- "I thought I had forgiven her, but the hurt has never gone away."
- "I'd rather just ignore her than deal with the issue."
- "She doesn't deserve forgiveness. What she did is so unimaginable I can't even think about it, let alone forgive her."
- "I'm not ready to forgive. It still hurts too much."

If these statements sound familiar to you, let this session be the first step toward healing. You cannot fully enjoy the blessings of friendships if you harbor resentment and refuse to forgive those who have hurt you.

1. List several ways that women hurt each other.

Why are those hurts so difficult to forgive?

Wounds from a friend cut deeper than those from an enemy ever could. In friendships, even comparably minor offenses are magnified under the lens of vulnerability. Honesty and vulnerability are essential qualities in any friendship, but they also increase your chances of being hurt by someone you've allowed to get close to you.

2. Why would God expect us to have open, honest relationships with others if that also means we have an increased chance of being hurt?

3. Have you ever been wounded by a close friend? Explain the situation and how it made you feel.

Although extending forgiveness to another may or may not make a difference to that person (there are those we must forgive who are long gone from our lives), that is not the primary reason we do it. Through forgiveness, we mend our own broken emotions—and in letting go, we deepen our relationship with God by giving Him our hurt.

4. In Matthew 18:21-35, was the master warranted in calling the servant wicked? Why or why not?

Reread verse 35. Why would God deal so harshly with those who refuse to forgive?

Jesus was betrayed by a friend, crucified by His countrymen and died on a cross for sins He didn't commit, yet He preached forgiveness and lived it out in His own life. Remembering the grace God has extended to us is foundational in being able to extend forgiveness to others.

5. What do each of the following passages have to say about the importance of forgiveness?

Matthew 6:12,14-15

Mark 11:25

Ephesians 4:31-32

If we refuse to obey God's commands to forgive someone who has sinned against us, we jeopardize our relationship with God. Any time we harbor sin in our heart, we block the lines of communication between us and God. Only admitting our sin and pursuing obedience will rectify our relationship with Him.

6. How does Romans 12:17-21 relate to forgiving others?

In what ways could you figuratively feed or offer a drink to someone who has hurt you?

7. Does forgiveness necessarily mean that your friendship with the person who has hurt you will be restored? Explain.

8. If you choose to forgive someone who has hurt you and that person accepts your forgiveness, what other obstacles might stand in the way of completely reconciling the friendship?

How might those obstacles be overcome?

Is a completely restored friendship always possible? Why or why not?

ENDURING HOPE

There is another aspect of forgiveness that brings incredible hope. The most common misconception about forgiveness is that we must forgive and forget.

The human mind doesn't work that way! Forgetting may be a by-product of forgiveness, but simply trying to block past offenses from our minds is never a means to forgiveness.

Some might attempt to forgive an offender by vowing never to remember the offense again. Then they feel discouraged and disillusioned when two years—or even two days—down the road, they feel a resurgence of bitterness and a desire to see justice met.

Their misconception follows this reasoning: *God has forgotten my sins, so I must forget the sins others commit against me.* But there is a problem with such reasoning. If God is omniscient—meaning He knows everything—can He ever completely *forget* anything?

9. Read the following Scripture passages and note what each says about God's omniscience.

   Psalm 139:1-4

   Isaiah 40:13-14

   Hebrews 4:13

If God knows everything, He certainly remembers what sins we committed last week! He has chosen to forgive us because Jesus paid the price for our sins on the cross at Calvary.

10. According to Psalm 103:10-12, what has God done instead of merely forgetting our sins?

   What does this tell you about the type of forgiveness you are to extend to others?

In Matthew 18:21-22, Peter asked, "Lord, how many times shall I forgive my brother when he sins against me? Up to seven times?" (v. 21). When Peter asked this question, he thought he was being generous. Some rabbis of the day—citing Amos 1:3,6,9,11,13—taught that since God forgave Israel's enemies only three times, forgiving anyone more than three times was unnecessary—and even presumptuous.[2] However, Jesus didn't think so.

11. According to Matthew 18:22, how did Jesus respond to Peter's question?

     Since Jesus' intent was obviously not to count each time we forgive another, what was He trying to teach Peter through His response?

     Even after we've extended forgiveness, there may still be times when we may want to scream, "Haven't I already dealt with this?" The Holy Spirit is powerful enough to wipe out all pain and bitterness once and for all, yet often He chooses not to, and our flesh battles resurgences of hurt and bitterness down the line.

     When Jesus told Peter to forgive no matter how many times someone sinned against him, perhaps He was thinking of those times when our flesh won't listen to us; when we relive those painful feelings day after day—sometimes hour after hour—for months, and sometimes years. Is it possible that He meant we are to forgive someone 70 times 7 times even *for the same offense?*

12. Have you ever battled resurgences of bitterness and/or pain for an offense you had already forgiven? Explain.

13. Read the parallel account of the Matthew passage in Luke 17:4-5. What was the apostles' response to Jesus' command to forgive numerous times?

When you feel the familiar pangs of hurt from an offense you've already decided to forgive, cry out to the Lord, "Increase my faith!" Remember, as you continue to choose obedience and think about what is true, your emotions will fall in line—maybe not today, or even this year, but you *will* experience complete healing through God's awesome power.

EVERYDAY LIFE

Think of those who have hurt you—whether one of your close friends or someone you haven't seen in ages. Before you answer the questions below, take a few minutes to ask the Lord to open your eyes and your heart and to reveal anyone in your life that you have not yet completely forgiven.

> *Dear Father, You have forgiven me for so much! I don't want to take Your grace for granted like the foolish servant in Matthew 18. Increase my faith that I may forgive from the heart. I desire to glorify You by extending to others just a fraction of the grace You have shown me. Clothe me in humility and give me the strength to do just that. Amen.*

For each person you still need to forgive (whether for the first time or the fiftieth time), use a separate piece of paper to answer the following questions. Write the initials of the person at the top of each page.

- What is keeping me from truly forgiving this person?
- For what words, attitudes or actions do I need to apologize?
- What steps can I take toward reconciling the relationship? (There may be none; if so, write the reason reconciliation isn't possible.)

- How can I specifically pray for this person?
- How can I show this person kindness?

When you have completed each piece of paper, pray about the relationship and ask for God's grace to forgive. May God's peace fill your heart and restore your friendships as you begin—or continue—the process of redeeming the wreckage unforgiveness has caused in your life. Remember, the journey may be difficult, but the benefits of reconciling a friendship are priceless.

Notes

1. This story is a fictional account. Any resemblance to actual events or people, living or dead, is purely coincidental.

2. John MacArthur, *The MacArthur Study Bible* (Nashville, TN: Word Bibles, 1997), p. 1426.

RESULT OF RIGHT
Relationships
THE BLESSINGS OF FRIENDSHIPS

How good and pleasant it is when brothers live together in unity!
For there the Lord bestows his blessing, even life forevermore.

PSALM 133:1,3

From him the whole body, joined and held together by every supporting ligament, grows and
builds itself up in love, as each part does its work.

EPHESIANS 4:16

E V E R Y D A Y   W O M A N

Every woman has a story to tell, and today it's your turn. In the space provided, write a brief true story about one of your relationships. For example, you could describe a time when a friend helped you through a difficult period or a time when a friend exemplified honesty, vulnerability or forgiveness.

Now let's take a look at what the Bible has to say about the blessings that come from healthy, right relationships.

ETERNAL WISDOM

God inspired many of the biblical writers to use illustrations, metaphors and word pictures to help us understand His messages. Paul used an interesting word picture to describe the relationships within the Body of Christ in 1 Corinthians 12:12-26.

1. How does Paul describe believers in this passage?

    Briefly summarize verses 15-24.

2. According to verses 24 and 25, why has God "given greater honor to the parts that lacked it"? What do you suppose this means?

3. What does verse 26 convey about relationships within the Body of Christ?

4. How are your physical body parts dependent on each other?

   In what ways are they independent of one another?

5. How are we as the Body of Christ dependent on one another?

   In what ways might we be independent of one another?

Although as members of Christ's Body we each retain an individual identity, we still work together through our unity and ministry for one purpose—to bring glory to the head of the body, Jesus Christ (see Ephesians 4:15).

6. According to Ephesians 4:16, how are the members of the Body of Christ connected?

What do you think the supporting ligaments signify?

Right relationships could be a part of the supporting ligaments in the Body of Christ. When we are held together by commitment, unconditional acceptance, honesty, vulnerability, forgiveness and respect, we grow and build each other up in love. That's the way God designed the Body to work, and as with all of His designs, this one results in immeasurable blessing and fulfillment.

ENDURING HOPE

One of the most important results of right relationships in the Body of Christ is unity. Unity allows us to work together to glorify God and share His love with others.

7. How is unity among believers described in Psalm 133?

David wrote this psalm as a picture of unity among the brethren of Israel—the descendants of Abraham, Isaac and Jacob. Now through His Son, Jesus Christ, God has extended to us as New Covenant believers not only the covenant He made with these patriarchs but also the blessings He promised.

Let's take a look at some of the blessings described in Psalm 133.

The first blessing we receive is likened to "precious oil poured on the head" (v. 2). Being covered in oil might not sound very enticing, but the spiritual symbolism is important.

8. According to Exodus 30:22-30, what was unique about the holy anointing oil? What did it contain?

What purpose did the oil serve (v. 29)?

9. Understanding the rich spiritual symbolism of the holy anointing oil, reread Psalm 133:2. How does the spiritual blessing of the oil apply to unity among believers?

The second blessing is likened to "the dew of Hermon . . . falling on Mount Zion" (v. 3). Mount Hermon is the largest mountain in Israel. It's located in the far northern region of the country and rises 9,200 feet in the air. It is so huge that the rain and snow runoff from the mountain forms hundreds of tiny streams that combine to create the Dan River, the most important of the three sources feeding into the Jordan River.[1] That's a lot of moisture, especially for such a relatively dry country! Now reread Psalm 133:3.

10. Jerusalem, or Mount Zion, receives an average rainfall of 20-30 inches per year and Mount Hermon receives 60 inches.[2] How might Jerusalem's landscape change if it were to receive the same amount of rainfall that Mount Hermon gets?

The picture David paints is one of refreshment—crystal clear streams, morning dew, winter snows and lush vegetation. If you've ever been to or seen pictures of Jerusalem, you can appreciate David's imagery!

11. How does this second blessing relate to unity and right relationships?

12. What third blessing is found in verse 3? How does it relate to unity?

We have much reason to sing with David, "How good and pleasant it is when brothers live together in unity!" (Psalm 133:1).

EVERYDAY LIFE

The past seven weeks have been filled with many lessons, experiences and blessings as we've explored the characteristics of true friendships. As this study comes to a close, take a moment to document your thoughts about each characteristic. You could comment on a lesson you've learned, an area you still need to work on, an insight you've gained or a way that someone has blessed you in that area. Briefly review each session if necessary. An example is given for the first session.

Characteristics of True Friendships	Personal Comments
Needed by women (session 1)	**Example:** *I had never realized why relationships were so important to women. As I've worked on building healthy friendships, I've felt much more fulfilled.*
Better when focused on a small core group (session 2)	
Encouraging (session 3)	
Honest and vulnerable (session 4)	
Characterized by listening (session 5)	
Opportunities for humility and growth (session 6)	
Based on forgiveness (session 7)	

Though Edgar Guest, known as the poet of the people, died in 1959, his down-to-earth poem "Be a Friend" transcends generations and captures much of what right relationships are all about.

BE A FRIEND

Be a friend. You don't need money;
Just a disposition sunny;
Just the wish to help another
Get along some way or other;
Just a kindly hand extended
Out to one who's unbefriended;
Just the will to give or lend,
This will make you someone's friend.
Be a friend. You don't need glory.
Friendship is a simple story.
Pass by trifling errors blindly,
Gaze on honest effort kindly,
Cheer the youth who's bravely trying,
Pity him who's sadly sighing;
Just a little labor spend
On the duties of a friend.
Be a friend. The pay is bigger
(Though not written by a figure)
Than is earned by people clever
In what's merely self-endeavor.
You'll have friends instead of neighbors
For the profits of your labors;
You'll be richer in the end
Than a prince, if you're a friend.[3]

13. Who has enriched your life with friendship? What could you do today to express your love for your friends?

Who is someone with whom you would like to develop a friendship? What first step could you make today toward making a new friend?

Abraham Lincoln once said, "The better part of one's life consists of his friendships."[4] May the same be true of your life, as God blesses you through the friendships you cultivate in the months and years to come.

Notes

1. "Tel Dan Nature Reserve," *Israel Nature and National Parks Protection Authority*. http://www.parks.org.il/ParksENG/company_card.php3?CNumber=508953 (accessed February 29, 2004).

2. "Seasons and Months in Palestine," *Geography and the Bible*. http://www.bible-history.com/geography/seasons_months_israel.html (accessed February 29, 2004).

3. Edgar Guest, "Be a Friend," *Poets' Corner*. http://www.theotherpages.org/poems (accessed February 29, 2004).

4. Bob Phillips, *Phillips' Awesome Collection of Quips and Quotes* (Eugene, OR: Harvest House Publishers, 2001), p. 172.

THE *Blessings* OF FRIENDSHIPS

General Guidelines

1. Your role as a facilitator is to get women talking and discussing areas in their lives that are hindering them in their spiritual growth and personal identity.

2. Be mindful of the time. There are four sections in each study. Don't spend too much time on one section unless it is obvious that God is working in people's lives at a particular moment.

3. Emphasize that the group meeting is a time to encourage and share with one another. Stress the importance of confidentiality—what is shared stays within the group.

4. Fellowship time is very important in building small-group relationships. Providing beverages and light refreshments either before or after each session will encourage a time of informal fellowship.

5. Encourage journaling as it helps women apply what they are learning and stay focused during personal devotional time.

6. Most women lead very busy lives; respect group members by beginning and ending meetings on time.

7. Always begin and end the meetings with prayer. If your group is small, have the whole group pray together. If it is larger than 10 members, form groups of 2 to 4 to share and pray for one another.

   One suggestion is to assign prayer partners each week. Encourage each group member to complete a Prayer Request Form as she arrives. Members can select a prayer request before leaving the meeting and pray for that person during the week. Or two women can trade prayer requests and then pray for each other at the end of the meeting and throughout the week. Encourage the women to call their prayer partner at least once during the week.

8. Another highly valuable activity is to encourage the women to memorize the key verse each week.

9. Be prepared. Pray for your preparation and for the group members during the week. Don't let one person dominate the discussion. Ask God to help you draw out the quiet ones without putting them on the spot.

10. Enlist the help of other group members to provide refreshments, to greet the women, to lead a discussion group or to call absentees to encourage them, etc. Whatever you can do to involve the women will help bring them back each week.

11. Spend time each meeting worshiping God. This can be done either at the beginning or the end of the meeting.

How to Use the Material

Suggestions for Group Study

There are many ways that this study can be used in a group situation. The most common way is a small-group Bible study format. However, it can also be used in a women's Sunday School class. However you choose to use it, here are some general guidelines to follow for group study:

- Keep the group small—8 to 12 participants is probably the maximum for effective ministry, relationship building and discussion. If you have a larger group, form smaller groups for the discussion time, selecting a facilitator for each group.
- Ask the women to commit to regular attendance for the eight weeks of the study. Regular attendance is a key to building relationships and trust in a group.
- Whatever is discussed in the group meetings is to be held in strictest confidence among group members only.

Suggestions for Mentoring Relationships

This study also lends itself for use in relationships in which one woman mentors another woman. Women in particular are admonished in Scripture to train other women (see Titus 2:3-5).

- A mentoring relationship could be arranged through a system set up by a church or women's ministry.
- A less formal way to start a mentoring relationship is for a younger woman or new believer to take the initiative and approach an older or more spiritually mature woman who exemplifies the Christlike life and ask to meet with her on a regular basis. Or the reverse might be a more mature woman who approaches a younger woman or new believer to begin a mentoring relationship.
- When asked to mentor, someone might shy away, thinking that she could never do that because her own walk with the Lord is less than perfect. But just as we are commanded to disciple new believers, we must learn to disciple others to strengthen their walk. The Lord has promised to be "with you always" (Matthew 28:20).
- When you agree to mentor another woman, be prepared to learn as much or more than the woman you will mentor. You will both be blessed by the mentoring relationship built on the relationship you have together in the Lord.

There are additional helps for mentoring relationships or leading small groups in *The Focus on the Family Women's Ministry Guide*.

THE ROLE OF RELATIONSHIPS:
Back to the Beginning

Before the Meeting
The following preparations should be made before each meeting:
1. Gather materials for making name tags (if women do not already know each other and/or if you do not already know everyone's name). Also gather extra pens or pencils and Bibles to loan to anyone who may need them.
2. Make photocopies of the Prayer Request Form (available in *The Focus on*

the *Family Women's Ministry Guide*), or provide 3x5-inch index cards for recording requests.

3. Read through your own answers and mark the questions that you especially want to have the group discuss.

Ice Breakers

1. Distribute Prayer Request Forms, or index cards, and ask each woman to at least write down her name, even if she doesn't have a specific prayer request. This way, someone can pray for her during the upcoming week. This can be done each week. Just because we don't have a specific prayer request doesn't mean we don't need prayer!

2. **Option A**—Introduce yourself and then share something unique about yourself. Have each woman in the group do likewise.

   Option B—Have each woman share one positive gift that she brings to her relationships (e.g., good listener, keeps in touch well, sympathetic to others).

Discussion

1. **Everyday Woman**—Discuss question 2 with the whole group.

2. **Eternal Wisdom**—Discuss question 3 and then review Eve's purpose and the effects the Fall had on both Adam and Eve. Have the women form groups of two or three to answer questions 5 through 9.

3. **Enduring Hope**—While still in small groups, have the women share their answers to questions 10 and 15. Gather the whole group and invite a volunteer from each group to share her group's answer to question 15. Invite volunteers to share general things that they learned from their answers to the more personal questions 11 through 14.

4. **Everyday Life**—Lead the group in a discussion about the result of placing other relationships ahead of our relationship with God. If the women in your group are familiar with each other, you might invite volunteers to share their answers to 17 or 18.

5. **Close in Prayer**—Lead the group in a closing prayer. As women prepare to leave, have each woman trade a Prayer Request Form with another woman and encourage the women to pray for one another during the week.

6. **Encourage Scripture Memory**—One very effective way to strengthen our relationship with God is to memorize His Word. Encourage the women to memorize the week's key verse or a verse from the lesson that was especially helpful for them. Provide an opportunity at each meeting for the women to recite their memory verses. *The Focus on the Family Women's Ministry Guide* contains additional information on encouraging Scripture memorization.

After the Meeting

1. **Evaluate**—Spend time evaluating the meeting's effectiveness (see *The Focus on the Family Women's Ministry Guide*, "Reproducible Forms" section for an evaluation form).
2. **Encourage**—During the week, try to contact each woman (through phone calls, notes of encouragement, e-mails or instant messages) and welcome her to the study. Make yourself available to answer any questions or concerns the women may have and generally get to know them. If you have a large group, enlist the aid of some women in the group to contact others.
3. **Equip**—Complete the Bible study.
4. **Pray**—Prayerfully prepare for the next meeting, praying for each woman and your own preparation. Discuss with the Lord any apprehension, excitement or anything else that is on your mind regarding the Bible study material or the group members. If you feel inadequate or unprepared, ask for strength and insight. If you feel tired or burdened, ask for God's light yoke. Whatever it is you need, ask God for it. He will provide!

RELATIONSHIPS 101:
The Perfect Model

Before the Meeting

1. Make the usual preparations as listed on pages 85-86.
2. Make the necessary preparations for the ice-breaker activity.
3. Have a white board or poster board and the appropriate felt-tip pens available for the teaching time.

Ice Breakers

1. Distribute Prayer Request Forms, or index cards, and encourage the women to write their names on the forms, even if they don't have any specific requests this week.
2. Invite volunteers to recite the memory verse, or recite it as a group.
3. Before everyone arrives, fill the following three types of containers (preferably clear glass) with the same measured amount of water: a rectangular baking dish; a large, shallow bowl; and a tall, slender vase.

    After everyone arrives, ask them which container contains the most water—the vase will have the illusion of having the most. Use this visual aid to lead into a discussion on spreading yourself too thin in relationships. Say something like the following: **Though we all have the same amount of "water" (time, energy and resources), how we choose to use it will determine how full, or fulfilled, we feel.**
4. Ask volunteers to share ways that a friend encouraged them this past week.

Discussion

1. **Everyday Woman**—Invite a few volunteers to share their answers to question 1. Discuss what they find most overwhelming about maintaining several relationships at once.
2. **Eternal Wisdom**—Briefly review the model for relationships that Christ

demonstrated during His visible ministry. Have the women form small groups of three or four women each to discuss questions 3 through 11. Then bring the whole group together and discuss question 13.

3. **Enduring Hope**—Discuss question 16. If your women's ministry doesn't have a formal mentoring program, this might be a good time to discuss starting one. *The Focus on the Family Women's Ministry Guide* has more information to help you develop a mentoring program.

4. **Everyday Life**—With the whole group, discuss the importance of commitment to friendship. Brainstorm ways in which we can encourage, teach and be fulfilled in meaningful relationships. Write the suggestions on a white board or poster board.

5. **Close in Prayer**—Have the women form pairs and pray for each other's relationships—that they will find fulfillment in a few, deeper friendships rather than many, shallow ones. Have these same partners exchange Prayer Request Forms, or index cards, for the week.

After the Meeting

1. **Evaluate.**
2. **Encourage.**
3. **Equip.**
4. **Pray.**

SESSION THREE–
REACHING OUT:
Encouraging Others

Before the Meeting

1. Make the usual preparations as listed on pages 85-86.
2. Make the necessary preparations for the ice-breaker activity you choose.
3. Make a large version of the encouragement chart in the Everyday Life section of this session. A large chalkboard, a white board or a roll of

white butcher paper will work best. List each woman in the group. If you have a group of more than eight women, you might consider forming smaller groups to complete the activity.

4. Gather a basket or other container for the Close in Prayer section.

Ice Breakers

1. Distribute Prayer Request Forms, or index cards, and remind women to write down their names, even if they don't have any specific requests this week.

2. Invite a volunteer to lead the other women in reciting the memory verse. Invite a volunteer to recite the verses from the previous sessions too.

3. **Option 1**—During the week, prepare a short note of encouragement for each woman in the group. These notes of encouragement don't have to be long or elaborate, but they should be personal. You may want to use nice stationery paper or note cards. No matter how well you know each woman, find at least one area in each woman's life about which you can encourage, comfort or compliment the woman.

   As the women arrive, hand them the personal notes that you prepared beforehand. After all the women have arrived, ask them how the notes made them feel; then briefly discuss the power of encouragement. **Option 2**—Invite volunteers to share how they applied the lesson of session 2.

4. Understanding the original context and meaning of the passages we study is important. Spend some time explaining why using Greek and Hebrew lexicons, as well as other study materials, can help us understand the Bible. Have at least one lexicon available for the women to browse through (you may be able to check out one from your church's library or borrow one from your pastor), and give a short demonstration on how to use a lexicon and other study materials (or invite a pastor or other guest to give the demonstration).

Discussion

1. **Everyday Woman**—Have the women share the proverbs they wrote for question 3. It may be helpful to share yours first.

2. **Eternal Wisdom**—Ask the women whether they have any questions

about the Greek words discussed in this section. Be especially mindful of women who aren't as familiar with the Bible, such as new Christians. Discuss questions 4 through 7. Invite volunteers to share their answers to question 8.

3. **Enduring Hope**—Form groups of three or four woman each and have each group develop a list in response to question 9. Then instruct the groups to briefly discuss questions 10 through 13. After a few minutes of discussion, have the groups share three ideas from their answers to question 9. Without giving names, invite volunteers to share their words of encouragement from the chart.

4. **Everyday Life**—Recreate the chart from page 34, adding enough rows for each woman in the group. Complete the chart with each woman's information. If time is short, you could have the chart ready at the beginning of the meeting and instruct the women to complete their personal information before the meeting begins. Encourage the women to copy the chart and to use the information to encourage others in the group during the remaining weeks of the study. Or have a volunteer take the information, reproduce it on her computer and distribute a copy to each woman at next week's meeting.

5. **Close in Prayer**—Lead the group in prayer, asking the Lord to teach each of you what it means to encourage others. Have each woman draw a Prayer Request Form, or index card, out of a basket and pray for the request during the week.

After the Meeting

1. **Evaluate.**
2. **Encourage.**
3. **Equip.**
4. **Pray.**

READY TO REVEAL:
Being Honest and Vulnerable

Before the Meeting

1. Make the usual preparations as listed on pages 85-86.
2. Make the necessary preparations for the ice-breaker activity.
3. Gather a basket or other container for the Close in Prayer section.

Ice Breakers

1. Distribute Prayer Request Forms, or index cards, and remind women to write down their names, even if they don't have any specific requests this week.
2. Invite a volunteer to lead the other women in reciting the memory verse. Invite a volunteer to recite the verses from the previous sessions too.
3. Give the women a few minutes to think of two true statements and one false one about themselves (personality, experiences, humorous accounts, etc.). As each woman shares her statements, the other women must decide which statement is false and write it on a piece of paper. When everyone has finished, find out which woman guessed the most false statements. Have a small prize for the winner. Briefly discuss why we put up a façade in front of others.

Discussion

1. **Everyday Woman**—Discuss questions 1 and 2.
2. **Eternal Wisdom**—The root hindrance to healthy vulnerability is pride. Discuss the different forms pride can take. Discuss question 3 and invite volunteers to share what sort of thorns in the flesh God has given them in the past (or present) to keep them humble. Discuss questions 4 through 9.
3. **Enduring Hope**—Have each woman read one of the "Vulnerability is" and "Vulnerability is not" statements on the chart and give an example.

Continue until the whole chart has been explained, coaching and adding comments when necessary. Invite volunteers to share their answer to question 12.

4. **Everyday Life**—Discuss the lies that Satan tries to feed women to keep us trapped in a cage of isolation and silence. Discuss: **What happens when we engage in mutual vulnerability? How can we be more vulnerable with one another?**

5. **Close in Prayer**—Form groups of three or four women each. Have the women pray for each other in the areas of honesty, humility and vulnerability. Place all the Prayer Request Forms, or index cards, in a basket or other container and have women draw a card as they leave.

After the Meeting

1. **Evaluate.**
2. **Encourage.**
3. **Equip.**
4. **Pray.**

SESSION FIVE–
RING! RING! ANYBODY HOME?:
The Fine Art of Listening

Before the Meeting

1. Make the usual preparations as listed on pages 85-86.
2. Make the necessary preparations for the ice-breaker activity.
3. Gather poster boards for the Enduring Hope and Everyday Life sections and a basket or other container for the Close in Prayer section.

Ice Breakers

1. Distribute Prayer Request Forms, or index cards, and remind the women to write down their names, even if they don't have any specific requests this week.

2. Invite a volunteer to lead the other women in reciting the memory verse. Invite a volunteer to recite the verses from the previous sessions too.

3. Before the meeting collect a phone, a coffee mug (with or without coffee), a large question mark cut out of paper, a watch and a box of tissues. Hand each item to a woman in the group. One by one, ask each woman to explain what her object might have to do with the art of listening.

Discussion

1. **Everyday Woman**—Say something like the following: **Were you more self-conscious this week about how much time you spent talking versus listening? I sure was! Isn't it amazing how self-centered we can become? Why do you think we have a tendency to act as if we had two mouths and only one ear?**

2. **Eternal Wisdom**—Discuss questions 2 through 6, focusing on the three stages of listening: hearing, considering and responding. Ask: **Why are women generally such poor listeners until we hear a juicy piece of gossip? Then we're all ears!** Discuss the importance of listening with discernment and refusing to entertain idle talk, inappropriate language or topics, gossip and blasphemy.

3. **Enduring Hope**—Explain: **Comforting those who are grieving or going through difficult situations is one of the greatest blessings we can offer them.** Discuss the mistakes Job's three friends made and the value of silence. Have the women brainstorm other ways to comfort those who are grieving. Write their ideas on a poster board. If there is someone in the group or someone that a woman in the group knows who is going through a rough time right now, make plans to implement the ideas on that person's behalf.

4. **Everyday Life**—Reiterate that the 2-Q test is an excellent way to show someone that you are interested in who she is and what she has to say. Ask: **What are some other ways we can communicate respect and genuine interest?** Spend the remaining time brainstorming ways to be

good listeners and good responders. You may want to write their ideas on a poster board for the group to keep as a reminder.

5. **Close in Prayer**—Lead the group in prayer, asking God to make each member of the group a good steward of the two ears and one mouth He has given her. Have women take a Prayer Request Form, or index card, from a basket or other container as they leave. Encourage them to contact their prayer partner at least once during the week.

After the Meeting

1. **Evaluate.**
2. **Encourage.**
3. **Equip.**
4. **Pray.**

SESSION SIX–
RECEIVING AND GIVING
CORRECTION:
Clothed in Grace and Humility

Before the Meeting

1. Make the usual preparations as listed on pages 85-86.
2. Make the necessary preparations for the ice-breaker activity.
3. Gather a magnifying mirror for the Enduring Hope section, a white board or poster board for the Everyday Life section and a basket or other container for the Close in Prayer section.

Ice Breakers

1. Distribute Prayer Request Forms, or index cards, and remind women to write down their names, even if they don't have any specific requests this week.

2. Invite a volunteer to lead the other women in reciting the memory verse. Invite a volunteer to recite the verses from the previous sessions too.

3. Cut out four or five pictures from a home-decorating magazine. Try to choose pictures that would cause people to have a strong opinion about the design—either loving or hating it (e.g., contemporary, country, traditional). Put each picture in a separate folder. Invite a volunteer to the front of the room, show her a picture and ask her to describe it for the group without making any judgments about it. For example, if she is describing a country-style room, she can't say "country" but she can name the things she sees in the picture: gingham-checked café curtains, farm tools, etc. Once the group has guessed the style of design, choose another volunteer and repeat the process using the remaining folders.

Discussion

1. **Everyday Woman—** Invite several volunteers to share their answers to the second part of question 1. Discuss the second part of question 2.

2. **Eternal Wisdom**—Discuss the quote from Elisabeth Elliot. Then discuss questions 3 through 6. Ask: **What other ways does the Lord discipline us?**

   Explain: **One of the most difficult things to accept is unmerited discipline.** Discuss the women's answers to question 9; then discuss questions 10 and 11. (The answers to question 11: sin, alone, one, two, the church, unbeliever.) Review the four elements of confrontation: ask, pray, confront and follow up. Ask if the women have any questions about these lists.

3. **Enduring Hope**—If possible, have a magnifying mirror available for a visual aid. Feel free to laugh together about our tendency to hide our blemishes. Ask: **What keeps us from wanting to know our faults?** Apply the women's answers to correction from others.

4. **Everyday Life**—On a white board or poster board, recreate the columns as explained in this section. Have a volunteer suggest a scenario in which someone needs to be confronted (or make up one yourself). Have the group complete the created chart using the suggested scenario.

5. **Close in Prayer**—Form groups of three or four women each. Have the women in each group pray for each other to be humble and teachable.

Place all the Prayer Request Forms, or index cards, in a basket or other container and have each woman draw a card as she leaves.

After the Meeting

1. **Evaluate.**
2. **Encourage.**
3. **Equip.**
4. **Pray.**

SESSION SEVEN–
REDEEMING THE WRECKAGE:
Forgiveness

Before the Meeting

1. Make the usual preparations as listed on pages 85-86.
2. Make the necessary preparations for the ice-breaker activity.
3. Make the necessary preparations for the Everyday Life activity and gather a basket or other container for the Close in Prayer section.

Ice Breakers

1. Distribute Prayer Request Forms, or index cards, and remind the women to write down their names, even if they don't have any specific requests this week.
2. Invite a volunteer to lead the other women in reciting the memory verse. Invite a volunteer to recite the verses from the previous sessions too.
3. Write the following quotations on poster boards and display them around the room. Discuss the quotations, asking the women if they agree or disagree and to explain their choice.

"The more a man knows the more he forgives."

—Catherine the Great[1]

"Forgiveness is the fragrance the violet sheds on the heel that has crushed it."

—Mark Twain[2]

"It is easier to forgive an enemy than to forgive a friend."

—William Blake[3]

"A Christian will find it cheaper to pardon than to resent. Forgiveness saves the expense of anger, the cost of hatred, the waste of spirits."

—Hannah More[4]

Discussion

1. **Everyday Woman**—Discuss question 1. Then ask why hurt is inevitable in relationships.

2. **Eternal Wisdom**—Ask: **Do you agree that we don't heal in order to forgive, but forgive in order to heal? Why or why not?** Discuss questions 2 and 4 through 8. Discuss: **Why is it important to ask forgiveness for any small sin you may have committed against someone who has hurt you?**

3. **Enduring Hope**—Discuss God's omniscience (question 9) and his forgiveness (question 10). Remind the women that the path to forgiveness begins with the disciples' words, "Increase our faith!" (Luke 17:5).

4. **Everyday Life**—Before the meeting, prepare small slips of paper for each woman in the group and gather pens or pencils. Lower the lights, light some candles and play meditative, soft music with a forgiveness theme if possible, but instrumentals will also work. During this time, invite the women to write on the slips of paper the initials of the people God brought to their minds as they worked through this section, as well as the offenses that were committed against them. After a time of prayer, destroy all the slips of paper in a fireplace or an outdoor barbeque or fire pit to signify forgiveness.

5. **Close in Prayer**—Lead the group in a time of thankful prayer, praising Jesus Christ for atoning for our sins and enabling us to forgive the

offenses of others that are so petty in comparison. Remind the women to take a Prayer Request Form, or index card, from the basket or container as they leave. Encourage them to contact their prayer partner at least once during the week.

After the Meeting

1. **Evaluate.**
2. **Encourage.**
3. **Equip.**
4. **Pray.**

Notes

1. Bob Phillips, *Phillips' Awesome Collection of Quips and Quotes* (Eugene, OR: Harvest House Publishers, 2001), p. 161.
2. Ibid., p. 162.
3. Ibid., p. 161.
4. Ibid., p. 162.

SESSION EIGHT–
RESULT OF RIGHT RELATIONSHIPS:
The Blessings of Friendships

Before the Meeting

1. Make the usual preparations as listed on pages 85-86.
2. Make the necessary preparations for the ice-breaker activity.
3. Make the necessary preparations for the Enduring Hope section and for the Everyday Life activity option you choose.
4. Make photocopies of the Study Review Form (see *The Focus on the Family Women's Ministry Guide*, "Reproducible Forms" section).

Ice Breakers

1. Distribute Prayer Request Forms, or index cards, and remind the women to write down their names, even if they don't have any specific requests this week.

2. Invite a volunteer to lead the other women in reciting the memory verse. Invite volunteers to recite the verses from all eight sessions. Be prepared with a gift for those who have memorized all eight verses.

3. Ask volunteers to share ways that they have grown through the course of this study. Allow ample time for this activity, as the main goal of today's session is to reflect on the ways each has grown.

Discussion

1. **Everyday Woman**—Before the meeting ask two to three women to share the stories they wrote for this section. Be sensitive and understanding if they decline. After sharing your story, give the volunteers the opportunity to share.

2. **Eternal Wisdom**—Discuss the metaphor of the body that Paul used to explain the Body of Christ; then briefly discuss questions 2 through 6.

   Form small groups of three or four women each and instruct each group to think of another analogy that describes the value of friendships. Have each small group share its analogy with the whole group.

3. **Enduring Hope**—Before the meeting, fill a small glass jar with olive oil and a drop of perfume and fill a pitcher with water. Also obtain a picture of Jerusalem (from a book or the Internet) and a basin. Read Psalm 133 aloud together; as you pass the jar around, ask: **What does the anointing oil symbolize?** Show the picture(s) of Jerusalem and ask: **Why would the dew of Hermon be such a blessing to the people of Zion?** Instruct the women to close their eyes and picture a desert. Slowly pour the pitcher of water into a basin, and then ask: **What words come to your mind as you hear the sound of the water? How do those words apply to the blessings of friendships and unity between sisters of Christ?**

4. **Everyday Life—Option 1:** On a large poster board or a white board, copy the chart from this section. Instruct the women to share the personal

comments that they wrote down for each characteristic of true friend-ships.

Option 2: This final activity is called Relationships Are like Pizza. It's meant to be fun and encouraging—the perfect way to end your study on relationships! The activity can be as simple or elaborate as you'd like to make it. For minimal effort, choose the first person on your right and say, **"If relationships were like pizza,** [state woman's name] **would be the** [state the pizza topping that best describes her personality and interests] **because . . ."** For example, "If relationships were like pizza, Monica would be the cheese because she holds everyone else together." You can use real pizza toppings, or you can make your own zany con-coction! If you have the time and energy, turn the activity into a mock cooking show, making an actual pizza as each topping is assigned and share it together afterwards (or keep a cooked pizza warm in the oven so that you can eat it right away). If you have a large group, have the women form groups of six to eight women each to do this activity.

5. **Close in Prayer**—As a group, thank the Lord for the many things He has taught each woman in the past several weeks about relationships. You may also choose to pray a special blessing on each woman present.

After the Meeting

1. **Evaluate**—Distribute the Study Review Forms for members to take home with them. Share about the importance of feedback, and ask members to take the time this week to write their review of the group meetings and then to return them to you.
2. **Encourage**—Contact each woman during the week to invite her to the next Focus on the Family Women's Series Bible study.
3. **Equip.**
4. **Pray.**

Welcome to the Family!

As you participate in the *Focus on the Family Women's Series*, it is our prayerful hope that God will deepen your understanding of His plan for you and that He will strengthen the women relationships in your congregation and community.

This series is just one of the many helpful, insightful, and encouraging resources produced by Focus on the Family. In fact, that's what Focus on the Family is all about—providing inspiration, information, and biblically based advice to people in all stages of life.

It began in 1977 with the vision of one man, Dr. James Dobson, a licensed psychologist and author of 18 best-selling books on marriage, parenting, and family. Alarmed by the societal, political, and economic pressures that were threatening the existence of the American family, Dr. Dobson founded Focus on the Family with one employee and a once-a-week radio broadcast aired on only 36 stations.

Now an international organization, the ministry is dedicated to preserving Judeo-Christian values and strengthening and encouraging families through the life-changing message of Jesus Christ. Focus ministries reach families worldwide through 10 separate radio broadcasts, two television news features, 13 publications, 18 Web sites, and a steady series of books and award-winning films and videos for people of all ages and interests.

We'd love to hear from you!

For more information about the ministry, or if we can be of help to your family, simply write to Focus on the Family, Colorado Springs, CO 80995 or call (800) A-FAMILY (232-6459). Friends in Canada may write Focus on the Family, PO Box 9800, Stn Terminal, Vancouver, BC V6B 4G3 or call (800) 661-9800. Visit our Web site—www.family.org—to learn more about Focus on the Family or to find out if there is an associate office in your country.

STRENGTHEN MARRIAGES.
STRENGTHEN YOUR CHURCH.
Here's Everything You Need for a Dynamic Marriage Ministry!

Group Starter Kit includes

- Nine Bible Studies: *The Masterpiece Marriage, The Passionate Marriage, The Fighting Marriage, The Model Marriage, The Surprising Marriage, The Giving Marriage, The Covenant Marriage, The Abundant Marriage* and *The Blended Marriage*
- *The Focus on the Family Marriage Ministry Guide*
- *An Introduction to the Focus on the Family Marriage Series* video

Focus on the Family®
Marriage Series
Group Starter Kit
Kit Box
Bible Study/Marriage
ISBN 08307.32365

The overall health of your church is directly linked to the health of its marriages. And in light of today's volatile pressures and changing lifestyles, your commitment to nurture and strengthen marriages needs tangible, practical help. Now **Focus on the Family—the acknowledged leader in Christian marriage and family resources**—gives churches a comprehensive group study series dedicated to enriching marriages. Strengthen marriages and strengthen your church with **The Focus on the Family Marriage Series.**